Declaration
of
Interdependence

POETRY BOOKS BY JANET WONG

Good Luck Gold

A Suitcase of Seaweed

The Rainbow Hand:
  Poems about Mothers and Children

Behind the Wheel:
  Poems about Driving

Night Garden:
  Poems from the World of Dreams

Knock on Wood:
  Poems about Superstitions

TWIST: Yoga Poems

Once Upon A Tiger:
  New Beginnings for Endangered Animals

The *PoetryTagTime* Anthologies
  PoetryTagTime
  P*TAG
  Gift Tag: Holiday Poems

Declaration
of
Interdependence

Poems for an Election Year

With a Voter's Journal
and
Discussion Guide

By Janet Wong

Cover Illustrations
by Julie Paschkis

www.PoetrySuitcase.com

PoetrySuitcase.com
4580 Province Line Road
Princeton, NJ 08540
info@PoetrySuitcase.com

Library of Congress Cataloging-in-Publication Data
is available.

ISBN-13: 978-1468191912
ISBN-10: 1468191918

TABLE OF CONTENTS

1 / LIBERTY

I pledge acceptance
of the views,
so different,
that make us America

To listen, to look,
to think, and to learn

One people
sharing the earth
responsible
for liberty
and justice
for all.

2 / WE THE PEOPLE

There's a crazy guy:

Scares kids on our street
kicks old dogs
pours oil down the drain
cusses loud about
e-v-e-r-y-thing
hates "wasting money"
on schools

And he has the right to vote.

Then there's me, just fifteen:

I worry about war
watch the 6 o'clock news
raise money for the poor
plant trees in the park

But where's my vote?

Yesterday
I filled out forms
for Grandma, Mom,
and Aunty Lin
to get their ballots
(absentee)—

And next month,
come election time,
I won't have a vote, no,
I'll have three:

Grandma,
Mom,
Aunty Lin
and me—

We are
We the People.

3 / SEED SPEECH

If you think
of words
as tiny seeds
that take root
and hold
this earth together

then you see
why it matters for us
to scatter even our smallest
thoughts out there,
to make our voices
heard—

There are no stupid questions.
And, yes:
there might be simple answers.

The birds are chirping:
more seeds,
more seeds!

4 / BILL OF RIGHTS

When the teacher
asked about the Bill of Rights
my friend said:

*Is that
when you get charged
for Free Speech?*

5 / Occupy the TV

I can't wait for the election
to be over, to be done.

This president selection:
99% no fun.

The cable TV coverage
occupies too many channels

With nonstop blah-blah-blabbing
by some not-so-expert panels.

They should call these things "Duh-baits,"
the way those guys are baited

Into acting so ridiculous
they seem uneducated.

I think they must be smarter.
They simply must know more

than they're showing us—say what?
You and me in '24?

6 / Once Upon A Time

Listen to old people
and it seems like

Once upon a time
the world was so different.

I wish
I could click the remote

And *poof!*
Instead of this boring nonsense

There would only be
Once Upon a Time:

Snow White for President!

7 / LAND OF THE FREE (KICK)

I do believe
beyond the shadow of a doubt
that I could vote for any
of twelve good men and women
to be president
if only they were willing
to have that job.
Brad and Angelina could job-share
and we'd be on top of the world.
Tebow: The Miracle President.
No one would mess with Oprah.
Or: how about my soccer coach?

With my soccer coach as president,
there would be no excuses.
Slack off and you'd have to do
fifty push-ups.
She could get Congress
playing together as a team.

God Bless America:
Land of the Free (Kick),
Home of the Brave!

8 / The Two-Party System

Winner
> *Loser*

Rich
> *Poor*

You're So "In"
> *Easy to Ignore*

Smooth Sweet Talker
> *Grouch Out of Touch*

Presidential
> *Thinks Too Much*

9 / THE WHOLE TEAM

The way things are
we're just looking
at the star quarterback,
when everyone knows
he can't win alone.

I want to see
how the whole team plays
together
before I place my bet.

10 / F WORDS
(for Kristin Rowe-Finkbeiner)

Father and his friend
are sitting by the fireplace
fighting over politics.
Fragments of their feud
float upstairs.
Something about:

foreign policy
feminism
facts
Fannie
Freddie
the Fed
fossil fuels
flip-flopping
frustration
failure—

a flurry of F words.

I want them to finish
by finding some
fixes.

#1 says:
That's a lie.

#2 says:
You can't hide.

#3:
Don't beat up on me.
The truth is just so . . .
complicated . . .
when you're trying to get
nominated.
My mind is fogged up
kind of hazy . . .
I know you think
it sounds plain crazy
but I simply don't remember.
Ask me again—

in December.

12 / RED STATES, BLUE STATES

Red?
Blue?

My neighborhood looks
purple polka-dotted
to me!

13 / SWING STATE

I heard them say on the TV
that we live in a swing state.

If we vote the right way
will our neighborhood
get a new playground?

14 / PRIMARIES AND CAUCUSES

Voting in a primary
is a multiple choice test—
simple subtraction
and process of elimination.
Shhhh! No talking!

Voting at a caucus
is a math contest
with a lot of word problems.
Convince the others
you know the answer.

15 / HOW DO YOU CHOOSE?

Uncle Al once told me
you can judge a man
by his shoes.
Practical?
Sturdy?
Or shiny and slick?

But of course it's not enough
to look at shoes
when you're choosing
a president.

Really.

We need a close look
at the socks, too.

Adam from Adams was running late.
Black Hawk Betty had a date.
Cole from Carroll got stuck at work.
Decatur Dave's dog went berserk.
Deb from Dubuque had a meal to prepare.
Linn's Linn decided to help with a prayer.
Muscatine Mike said: "I'm just one."
Sioux City's Sue: "Losing's no fun."

Eight for Santorum stayed home Caucus Night.
And Romney won—by 8, all right. *

*Until someone saw the numbers and said,
"I know those numbers aren't what I read
on the piece of paper we handed in.
Santorum had more. Um . . . let's count again."
Though ballots had been destroyed, long gone,
a partial recount was done. And Strawn,
the GOP boss, said the loss by 8
was a win by 34—no, wait—
not really a win: a "split decision," a tie.
Santorum supporters questioned why
and the next night Strawn "clarified";
poor Mitt Romney must have cried.

Oh, and: Adam from Adams (who ran late)
has quite a story. His long-distance mate
was blogging about voting for Stephen Colbert.
"You couldn't," he said. "His name wasn't there!"
Adam's wife said, "There was nobody finah
for Prez of the U.S. of South Carolina."

Indeed she did vote for Colbert (or Cain)
and it wasn't entirely a vote cast in vain:
for Stephen (as Herman) won 1 percent,
a tiny but audible vote of dissent.
Adam from Adams said, "This takes the cake—
when the best choice you have is only a fake."

17 / MAKE YOUR BALLOT COUNT

Darken the circles completely
(neatly, not outside the lines).

If you don't know what to do
ask the helpers (follow the signs).

When you punch the holes, be firm
(no worm-like hanging chad).

When your vote is done,
your vote is gone.

A wrong vote? That's too bad.
A wasted vote: so sad.

18 / Electoral Math

50,456,002 > 50,999,897?
100,455,899 = 538
270 = Winner!

19 / WINNERS AND LOSERS

I was excited for a minute—
I thought my guy could win it!
But
he's been defeated.
I'm a deflated tired balloon.
Can't stand the winner.
Don't feel like eating dinner.
I'm worried about our country.
Is our future doomed?

Mom says: the country's fine—
but can you clean your room?

20 / Declaration of Interdependence

We hold these truths
to be not-so-self-evident—
but think about them a while
and you might agree:

all men are created equal-
ly a puzzle, made up
of so many parts;
and each of us makes up part

of the greater puzzle
that is our nation.
Lose one piece
and the picture is incomplete.

What happens when
too many pieces,
one by one,
become lost?

Life, Liberty, and the pursuit
of Happiness: let's do our best
to find the pieces that fit together,
to make our picture whole.

AUTHOR'S NOTE

I am not into politics. Civil liberties, human rights, social justice—these are good words, but they always have been just words to me. Some people go absolutely crazy, foaming at the mouth, with talk about the Constitution. I would rather talk about puppies.

I feel angry when I hear about unfairness and bigotry, the powerful taking advantage of the weak. The thing is, though, I have never witnessed anything horrible. I have never seen someone beaten bloody, tortured to talk. In other parts of the world, you might get your tongue cut off for speaking truth that the police did not want to hear. Lose your hand without so much as a trial. In other parts of the world, a twelve-year-old girl might be sold as a bride, to pay off her family's debt. If I lived in a place like that, I bet I would be more political. But I live in the suburbs of New Jersey. My biggest problems are bad air conditioning and too much traffic. Wait: Maybe these are my biggest problems because I live in a place where the government allows people to foam at the mouth over the Constitution.

What would happen if I went to the super-market and there were only two checkout lines, one for men and one for women? In another country, the people in power might say, "So what?" In this country, our civil liberties give us voice. We can complain, we can picket, we can sue, we can shut the store down. Separate is not equal in that context. What would happen if I went to the doctor with a serious condition that would change my life forever—but the doctor was afraid to help me because it was against the law? I would ask, "Is that law justified?" In this country, we can challenge unconstitutional laws.

I hope my words inspire you to look around, to read the papers, to talk about what's going on in the world, to vote (or encourage people to vote)—and to take the initiative to contribute, in your own best way.

Acknowledgments

I am grateful for the many friends who have inspired me to follow their example of staying informed about politics and taking action. Extra special thanks to three of these friends, in particular: Julie Paschkis, who provided the painting for the cover of this book, and whose "Liberty Notes" planted the seed of this project in my mind; Elaine Magliaro, who entertains and inspires with her Political Verses, and whose feedback helped shape this manuscript; and April Halprin Wayland, fellow poet and passionate political organizer, fundraiser, and volunteer.

You all have my vote in anything you want to do!

ABOUT THE AUTHOR

Janet Wong was born and raised in California, the child of Korean and Chinese immigrants. She obtained a B.A. in History from UCLA and a J.D. from Yale Law School. Janet worked for a few years as a lawyer, then decided to write full-time for children and teens. Her work has a wide range, including picture books, chapter books, poetry collections, and books about writing.

Janet's poems have been featured in some unusual venues, including a car-talk radio show and on 5,000 subway and bus posters as part of the New York City Metropolitan Transit Authority's "Poetry in Motion" program. She has been featured on The Oprah Winfrey Show and CNN, and has read her books at the White House. Janet's most recent collection of poetry is *Once Upon A Tiger: New Beginnings for Endangered Animals*.

http://www.janetwong.com

A Voter's Journal
AND
DISCUSSION GUIDE

A Voter's Journal

Here are some discussion and writing ideas for you.

If a question inspires you, jot down a few notes. Write more later. Talk your ideas over with a friend.

And post your ideas—whether you're 9 years old or 90—join the discussion at The Declaration Of Interdependence Blog:

TheDeclarationOfInterdependenceBlog. blogspot.com

Hope to see you there!

THE FIRST ELECTION YOU REMEMBER

What do you remember?

Was it an election where you were a volunteer? An election you heard a lot about from your parents? A school election for student government or an election for a team captain?

Ask A Voter

Ask your grandparents, parents, another family member, or a neighbor about an election that was important to them.

GET OUT THE VOTE!

What would you say to convince someone that his vote counts?

IMPOSSIBLE

Write a list of 10 impossible things that you would
want to do if you were president.

POSSIBLE

Write a list of 10 possible things you could do as president—promises that you could make (and might have a good chance of keeping).

Ridiculous

Write a list of the most ridiculous (or scariest or most impractical) ideas you've heard from presidential candidates (official and unofficial).

Write a list of the most inspiring or sensible ideas
you've heard from presidential candidates (official
or unofficial) in this election.

WOOF!

If you were a dog, what kinds of promises would
you want to hear from your mayor?

THE TREE GOVERNOR

What if you were a tree? What would you want
your governor to believe?

WHO'S THE WINNER?

Predict the winner of the next presidential
election. Will you be happy if you're right? If so,
how can you help make it happen? If not, what can
you do?

WHO WOULD YOU WANT?

Who would be some of your ideal presidential
candidates? Why?

Your Own Pledge

Using "Liberty" as your inspiration, write your own Pledge here.

JOIN THE DISCUSSION

POST YOUR IDEAS

BECOME PART OF OUR COMMUNITY

AT

THEDECLARATIONOFINTERDEPENDENCEBLOG.
BLOGSPOT.COM

AND

V O T E !

Made in the USA
Charleston, SC
06 February 2012